7

# About Alice

# About Alice

## CALVIN TRILLIN

RANDOM HOUSE   NEW YORK

Published in the United States by Random House,
an imprint of The Random House Publishing Group,
a division of Random House, Inc., New York.

RANDOM HOUSE and colophon are registered trademarks
of Random House, Inc.

This book originally appeared,
in somewhat shorter form, in *The New Yorker.*

ISBN 978-1-4000-6615-5

LIBRARY OF CONGRESS CATALOGING-IN-PUBLICATION DATA

Trillin, Calvin.
About Alice / Calvin Trillin.
p.      cm.
ISBN-13: 978-1-4000-6615-5
ISBN-10: 1-4000-6615-8
1. Trillin, Calvin—Marriage.   2. Trillin, Alice Stewart.
3. Authors' spouses—United States—Biography.   4. Cancer—Patients—Biography.
5. Authors, American—20th century—Biography.   I. Title.
PS3570.R5Z46 2007
814'.54—dc22      2006045573

Printed in the United States of America on acid-free paper

www.atrandom.com

68975

*Book design by Carole Lowenstein*

*For our grandchildren—*
*Izzy and Toby and Rebecca and Nate*

# About Alice

# I

*Now that it's fashionable to reveal intimate details*
*of married life, I can state publicly that my wife, Alice,*
*has a weird predilection for limiting*
*our family to three meals a day.*

—Alice, Let's Eat

There was one condolence letter that made me laugh. Naturally, a lot of them made me cry. Some of those, oddly enough, were from people who had never met Alice. They had become familiar with her as a character in books and magazine pieces I'd written—light books and magazine pieces about traveling or eating or family life. Virtually all those letters began in the same way, with a phrase like "Even though I never really knew Alice. . . ." I was certain of what Alice's response would have been. "They're right about that," she would have said. "They never knew me."

I once wrote that tales about writers' families tend to have a relation to real life that can be expressed in terms of standard network-television fare, on a spectrum that goes from sitcoms to Lifetime movies, and that mine were sitcoms. Now that I think of it, maybe they were more like the Saturday-morning cartoons. Alice played the role of the mom—the voice of reason, the sensible person who kept everything on an even keel despite the antics of her marginally goofy husband. Years ago, at a conference of English teachers where we were both speakers, the professor who did the introductions said something like "Alice and Bud are like Burns and Allen, except she's George and he's Gracie." Yes, of course, the role she played in my stories was based on the role she played in our family—our daughters and I sometimes called her T.M., which stood for The Mother—but she didn't play it in the broad strokes of a sitcom mom. Also, she was never completely comfortable as the person who takes responsibility for keeping things on an even keel; that person inevitably misses out on some of the fun. ("I feel the need to break out of the role of straight person," she said in a *Nation* review of *Alice, Let's Eat* that cautioned readers against abandoning long-planned European vacations in order to scour the country for "the perfect roast polecat haunch.") The sitcom presentation sometimes made her sound stern as well as wise, and she was anything but stern. She had something close to a child's sense of wonderment. She was the only adult I ever knew who might respond to encountering a deer on a forest path by saying, "Wowsers!"

Once, during a question-and-answer period that followed a speech I had given at the Herbst Theatre, in San Francisco, someone asked how Alice felt about the way she was portrayed in my books and articles. I said that she thought the portrayal made her sound like what she called "a dietitian in sensible shoes." Then the same questioner asked if Alice was in the audience, and, when I said she was, he asked if she'd mind standing up. Alice stood. As usual, she looked smashing. She didn't say anything. She just leaned over and took off one of her shoes—shoes that looked like they cost about the amount of money required in some places to tide a family of four over for a year or two—and, smiling, waved it in the air. She wasn't a dietitian in sensible shoes, and she would have been right in saying that the people whose exposure to her had been through my stories didn't know her. Still, in the weeks after she died I was touched by their letters. They may not have known her, but they knew how I felt about her. It surprised me that they had managed to divine that from reading stories that were essentially sitcoms. Even after I'd taken in most episodes of *The Honeymooners*, after all, it had never occurred to me to ponder the feelings Ralph Kramden must have had for Alice Kramden. Yet I got a lot of letters like the one from a young woman in New York who wrote that she sometimes looked at her boyfriend and thought, "But will he love me like Calvin loves Alice?"

The letter that made me laugh was from Roger Wilkins. By the time of Alice's death, Roger occupied a chair of history and American culture at George Mason University, but in the seventies he had been on the editorial board of *The New York Times*. In that period, I'd sometimes join the regular lunches he had with the late Richard Harris—a remarkable investigative reporter for *The New Yorker* who had the aggressively unsentimental worldview often found among people in his line of work. Alice and Roger became acquainted when she accompanied me to a conference I was covering in New Orleans. In off hours, when we'd gather around the hotel swimming pool, she and Roger sometimes had long, serious conversations. It wasn't unusual for me to find Alice having long, serious conversations with people I'd been bantering with for years. She got engaged with people's lives. If she said to a friend's son or daughter, "How's school?" she wasn't just being polite; she wanted details, and she wasn't shy about offering advice. If people we were visiting mentioned that they'd been thinking about renovating their house, Alice was right on the case, room by room. In such architectural conversations, she could get bossy, and sometimes I felt obliged to warn our hosts that one of her characteristic gestures—the gesture she used when she was saying something like "You have to open all of this up"—was remarkably similar to the gesture you'd use to toss money into the wind.

She wasn't among those whose response to tragedy or loss was limited to offering the conventional expressions of sympathy before moving on with their own lives. In 1988, an old friend phoned us to say that his grown daughter, a young woman we'd known since she was a child, had been raped by an intruder. This was a dozen years after Alice had been operated on for lung cancer, and among the things that she wrote to our friend's daughter was that having lung cancer and being raped were comparable only in that both were what she called "realizations of our worst nightmares." She said that there was some relief at surviving what you might have thought was not survivable. "No one would ever choose to have cancer or to be raped," she wrote. "But you don't get to choose, and it is possible at least to understand what Ernest Becker meant when he said something like 'To live fully is to live with an awareness of the rumble of terror that underlies everything,' or to begin to understand the line in 'King Lear'—'Ripeness is all.' You might have chosen to become ripe less dramatically or dangerously, but you can still savor ripeness." Alice had a large envelope in which she kept copies of letters like that—along with copies of some letters she had sent the girls and copies of poems we had written for her on birthdays and documents like the announcement of a prize for community service that Abigail, our older daughter, had been awarded at Yale and an astonishing letter of recommendation that a professor had provided for Sarah, our younger daughter, when she applied for her first job after getting her M.S.W. On the envelope was written "Important Stuff."

In his condolence letter, Roger talked partly about that engaged quality in Alice, but he also got around to her appearance. "She was nice and she was concerned and she was smart and when she talked to you, she was thinking about you, and, also, she was so very pretty," he wrote in September of 2001, a few days after Alice died. "I always thought of you as a wonderful guy, but still I couldn't figure out how you managed to get Alice. Harris once told me it was just dumb luck." When I read that, I burst out laughing. Harris had nailed it again.

# II

*When approached by young people in search of*
*wisdom about how they might go about linking up with*
*someone with whom they are likely to enjoy*
*a long and happy marriage, the only strategy*
*I can divine from what passed for my wife-seeking*
*activities is "Wander into the right party."*

—Family Man

The party was thrown in late 1963 by *Monocle,* a doomed magazine of political satire. *Monocle*'s parties seemed to grow more elaborate as its financial situation became increasingly bleak. Three or four other couples with connections to *Monocle* met and eventually married; those unions, which we called "*Monocle* marriages" in our house, were all long-lasting. I have reminded the founder of *Monocle*—Victor Navasky, who is fortunate enough to have a *Monocle* marriage himself—that his brainchild proved to be more durable as a marriage brokerage than as a magazine. In Alice's view, *Monocle* had existed in order to get everyone married, a project that might well require larger and larger parties, and, once that had occurred, it quite naturally folded.

When I saw Alice at that *Monocle* party, she was wearing a hat. At least, I've always remembered her as wearing a hat. She later insisted that she'd never owned a hat of the sort I described. Maybe, but I can still see her in the hat—a white hat, cocked a bit to the side. Her cheeks were slightly flushed. She had blond hair, worn straight in those days, and a brow just a shade darker than her hair. (Our oldest grandchild, Isabelle Alice, who was born in 2002, has precisely that coloring, which may be one reason I sometimes have trouble taking my eyes off her.) Whether or not Alice was wearing a hat was not the only difference in the way we recalled that meeting.

Alice's father had grown up in rural North Carolina, in a Southern Baptist family named Stewart, but her mother was Jewish—a fact that was to come as a great relief to my own Jewish mother, once I reminded her that, according to the ancient Hebraic belief in matrilineal descent, anyone whose mother was Jewish is herself Jewish. Although some people thought that Alice looked like the quintessential *shiksa*, I always claimed that when I spotted her across the room that night I asked Navasky, "Who's that cute little Jewish girl over by the punch bowl?" Alice always said that I'd made up that story and that, furthermore, there wasn't any punch bowl.

She was, as Roger Wilkins later wrote, so very pretty, but that wasn't the first thing that struck me about her; it might have come as much as two or three seconds later. My first impression was that she looked more alive than anyone I'd ever seen. She seemed to glow. For one reason or another, I barely got to speak to her that evening. Two weeks later, though, after doing some intelligence work and juggling some obligations and dismissing as hearsay the vague impression of one mutual acquaintance that

Alice was virtually engaged, I dashed back from a remote suburb to a party that I figured she'd be attending. So I couldn't claim that I just wandered into that second party; in romantic matters, even those who need to depend mainly on dumb luck are usually up to one or two deliberate moves. At the second party, I did get to talk to her quite a lot. In fact, I must have hardly shut up. I was like a lounge comic who had been informed that a booker for *The Tonight Show* was in the audience. Recalling that party in later years, Alice would sometimes say, "You have never again been as funny as you were that night."

"You mean I peaked in December of 1963?" I'd say, twenty or even thirty years later.

"I'm afraid so."

But I never stopped trying to match that evening—not just trying to entertain her but trying to impress her. Decades later—after we had been married for more than thirty-five years, after our girls were grown—I still wanted to impress her. I still knew that if I ever disappointed her in some fundamental way—if I ever caused her to conclude that, after all was said and done, she should have said no when, at the end of that desperate comedy routine, I asked her if we could have dinner sometime—I would have been devastated.

A year before Alice died, I read an obituary in *The New York Times* of Mary Francis, who had been married to the English mystery novelist Dick Francis for fifty-three years. "I don't think I shall write again other than letters now," Dick Francis was quoted as saying. "So much of my work was her." Apparently, Mary Francis had been such an active participant in her husband's work, particularly in the matter of research, that he considered the novels a joint effort. She had been well educated, and Dick Francis was conscious of being a novelist who had left school at fifteen to become a jockey. The article implied that he might not be able to produce a book without her help. But I read his reluctance to write novels without her another way. As I understood what he was saying, she was the one he'd been trying to impress.

I showed Alice everything I wrote in rough draft— partly because I valued her opinion but partly because I hoped to impress her. If the piece was meant to be funny, the sound of laughter from the next room was a great reward. The dedication of the first book I wrote after I'd met her, a collection of comic short stories, said, until I decided that the last few words were too corny, "These stories were written for Alice—to make her giggle." When I wrote in the dedication of a book "For Alice," I meant it literally. In that sense, the headline on her obituary in the *Times* was literally true, as well as in the correct order: it described her as "Educator, Author and Muse." When Alice died, I was going over the galleys of a novel about parking in New York—a subject so silly that I think I would have hesitated to submit the book to a publisher if she hadn't, somewhat to her surprise, liked it. When the novel was published, the dedication said, "I wrote this for Alice. Actually, I wrote everything for Alice."

# III

A Conversation with Someone
Who Can't Believe That Alice Is Fifty

*"No way," you say.*
*"It simply cannot be.*
*I would have guessed*
*That barmen often ask her for I.D."*
*"I know, I know.*
*She has that youthful glow*
*That still gives young men vapors.*
*She's fifty, though.*
*I've seen her papers."*

—Family Man

It had never occurred to me that being pretty involved complications. It wasn't the sort of problem I'd ever had to face. Of course, there are also plenty of advantages to being pretty. I once wrote that when we were in Italy I always referred to Alice as *la principessa* because it tended to improve the service in hotels, but she was often treated like a princess even when I hadn't implied a royal connection. Like a lot of attractive women, she regularly drove over the speed limit, secure in the knowledge that every policeman who had ever stopped her for speeding had given her a warning rather than a summons. At parties, she often attracted what I called "guys smoking pipes," who wanted to impress her with their suavity or intellectual range. "He wasn't smoking a pipe, by the way," she'd say, knowing just which guy I was talking about when I mentioned "that guy with a pipe" as we discussed a party on the way home. "In fact, I can't remember any of those 'guys smoking pipes' who actually were smoking pipes."

"Is that right?" I'd say. "I could have sworn he was tamping down the tobacco, or whatever they do, when he made that remark about the flaws in Derrida's thinking."

I wasn't surprised that Alice attracted guys with pipes. They didn't mean any harm, and I'm hardly in a position to criticize people for trying to impress her. What did surprise me—it still puzzles me—was that some men were hostile to her before she'd said any more than "Nice to meet you." Every once in a while, some man who'd just met Alice—I remember a lawyer in the South of France, for instance, and a financier in Manhattan—seemed intent on being contentious or even offensive from the start. In *St. Urbain's Horseman*, which may be my favorite Mordecai Richler novel, the protagonist assumes that men who responded offensively to the beautiful woman he married were "wreaking vengeance for a rejection they anticipated but were too cowardly to risk." That might have explained why some men seemed angry at the sight of Alice, but it didn't explain the response of others—the lawyer in France, for instance, who was gay. Why would he be interested in some sort of preemptive strike?

It was easier to explain the quieter but more common hostility from some women. Not long after we were married, I told Alice I'd noticed something about her response to couples we met: when she said something like

"That was fun; I hope we see them again," the female half of the couple was likely to be, in addition to her other qualities, physically attractive. I had been under the impression—an impression that I'd probably picked up from Hollywood movies about Hollywood—that the presence of two particularly attractive women at dinner produced a competitive tension that could interfere with digestion. "Do you feel more comfortable with attractive women because you don't have to worry about being resented?" I asked. She looked at me as if I'd intruded on something that was meant to be private.

The normal complications of prettiness were exacerbated by the fact that Alice didn't look like who she was. At first meeting, her looks—particularly when coupled with clothes of the sort that no dietitian had ever worn and the superficial facts of her background (Westchester County, Wellesley)—could make people expect someone who acted pampered or snooty. Among people who went to public high schools in the fifties, as we both did, pretty girls weren't expected to be smart or even especially nice. Pretty was enough. Alice always insisted that in high school she wasn't known as the class beauty but, embarrassingly enough, as the class brain—an embarrassment that was memorialized in her high-school yearbook by the pairing of her picture with a picture of the smartest boy in the class, a geeky slide-rule specialist in the days before the computer age saved geeky boys from eternal damnation. She often mentioned that in high school she'd been rejected at the cheerleading tryouts year after year and that, presumably because of her reputation as the class brain, she was virtually never asked out.

Her parents hadn't been able to afford any serious pampering. She grew up among prosperous suburbanites in a family that was always in precarious shape financially. Her father, who had left North Carolina as a teenager and never returned, was an inventor, self-taught. In the thirties, he had hit the jackpot with some early coin-changers for vending machines. He got an office in the Empire State Building, where, as it happened, Alice's mother was working in the secretarial pool. They bought a large stone house, with an elaborate swimming pool and a basement bowling alley, in Greenhaven—

an expensive Westchester community on Long Island Sound whose residents, in Alice's childhood memories, were exquisitely conscious of their material possessions and of having a couple of neighbors whose names resonated in Hollywood. But the company Alice's father founded to manufacture and market his inventions went under at about the time she was born. He never hit the jackpot again. As far as I can tell, he got by after that mostly with research-and-development money from a series of investors. Until the Stewarts moved to a more modest place, in Harrison, when Alice was about thirteen, they held on to the big house only by renting it during the summer while Alice went to a sleep-away camp, chosen partly for its reasonable fees, and her parents lived in a sublet apartment.

I've always thought that it must be sadder to be a businessman without money than, say, a poet without money or a coal miner without money. You've failed at the very game you signed up to play. Alice's father never lost his faith in the game, and he seemed confident that it was only a matter of time before he made a comeback.

Unwilling to have his daughter on scholarship, he worked out a monthly pay schedule for her Wellesley tuition. He was a sweet man—too openhearted, I suppose, to be in business. He was enormously optimistic, a quality that Alice thought she'd inherited pretty much intact. "You said that much of what appears to be optimism is actually denial," she once wrote our younger daughter, Sarah. "You are right about this. My dad was in denial much of the time." Once, after Alice's father was too old to be chasing investors who shared his dreams about, say, a vending machine for dispensing *Playboy* magazines, he and Alice's mother, who was then slipping into what turned out to be early-onset Alzheimer's, had a serious house fire. It was a disaster that followed a series of setbacks, all of which Alice had somehow managed to straighten out. I remember him patting Alice on the hand the day after the fire and saying, "I don't want you to worry about anything, sweetie." I know he genuinely meant it, even though if Alice had not worried about anything he would have been a goner.

When we were in our early thirties, it occurred to me

that one way to divide the people we knew was that some of them were still dependent on their parents—financially or emotionally or some other way—and some of them had seen that role ended or even reversed. I never embarked on a study to see if that distinction was a predictor of how people handled what has to be handled to get through life—the small matters of logistics and maintenance that were known around our house as Administrative Caca, or serious issues of, say, catastrophic illness or financial disaster—but I suppose I always assumed that Alice's early responsibility for her parents had something to do with her tendency to sit down and systematically deal with whatever problem came up. By the time I met her—she was in her mid-twenties then, teaching English at Hofstra University—she had already taken out bank loans to tide her father over when there was a dry period between investors. In the late seventies, she wrote an article about her parents that began, "When my daughter Abigail was three and my mother was sixty-three, Abigail said to me, 'Mommy, why is it that sometimes you seem like the mommy and Grandma seems like the little girl?' " As the health and finances of her parents crumbled over the years, Alice, their only child and nearly their only relative, acquired a lot more experience in keeping a family on an even keel than any sitcom mother ever needed.

Usually, she was also involved in taking care of someone else—a former student who couldn't find a job or a friend who was having difficulty coping or a great-aunt who couldn't manage to work through the maze required to become eligible for Medicaid or, increasingly, someone who was trying to deal with the terrors and bewildering logistics of being treated for cancer. There were so many cancer patients, and Alice's involvement in their cases was so complete, that I half expected a man from the New York State Board of Regents to walk in one day and accuse her of practicing medicine without a license. At Alice's memorial service, our friend Nora Ephron described those under Alice's protection as "anyone she loved, or liked, or knew, or didn't quite know but knew someone who did, or didn't know from a hole in a wall but had just gotten a telephone call from because they'd found the number in the telephone book."

Sometimes, noticing the sour expression of a woman sitting across a table from us, I wanted to say, "It's not Alice's fault how she looks," but that wouldn't have been quite true. She took some care to look pretty. She was quite aware of what she looked like: listening to the reminiscences of Alice and her college classmates, I got the impression that at Wellesley everyone knew precisely who the three most beautiful young women in the class were, in the way everyone might have known precisely who the three best bridge players were. She liked being pretty, usually. Who wouldn't? Traffic policemen are not the only people who tend to respond differently to a pretty woman.

A couple of years after Sarah was born—Alice would have been thirty-five—someone we knew was, for his sins, put in charge of a fashion issue of the *Times Magazine*, and he decided to skip professional models in favor of working women, who would be pictured wearing the new spring lines. The editor asked Alice if she'd be willing to be included. The customary promises were made about the marvelous prints we'd get of the pictures that a well-known photographer, Doug Kirkland, would take of Alice and maybe of Abigail and Sarah as well. Although Alice had been in similar spreads in college, she had some misgivings. Eventually, she agreed to participate, partly because the embarrassment potential of the accompanying article was somewhat limited by the fact that I was to write it. (In it, I said that, since I'd never seen Alice read a fashion magazine, the fact that she was able to answer in detail when I asked her about someone's bizarre outfit always stunned me, "as if I had idly wondered out loud about the meaning of some inscription on some ruin in Oaxaca and she had responded by translating fluently from the Toltec.") The *Times* headline said "College instructor, mother and wife."

Later, when writing about how dealing with her parents' problems sometimes made her feel as helpless as she had felt as a child, she said, "When some pictures of me and my children appeared in the fashion section of the *Times*, I found that although I was uncomfortable at the thought that any of my students might see such a frivolous portrayal of me, I was anxious that some of the doctors who had condescended to me over the phone see what a truly acceptable person I was. I even brought an extra copy of the magazine to my father so that he could show it to the people at the nursing home where he and my mother were then living, as if the nurses would respond more quickly to their calls if they had seen their daughter in the *Times*. And I believed they would have. Because when dealing in this area I was reduced to the values of Greenhaven in about 1948, when I was ten."

We did indeed get some nice prints from the photo shoot. One of them is still on my bedside table. It's a portrait of Alice in a hat. That was not the picture on the cover of the program at her memorial service. The picture on the program—chosen because I knew it was one of Alice's favorites—was taken on a trip to Italy to celebrate her fiftieth birthday. Eleven years after that trip, I wrote a sequel to her fiftieth-birthday poem called "An Explanation to Someone Who Still Finds It Hard to

Believe Alice Is Fifty—Eleven Years Later." The first
stanza was:

"*You josh, by gosh,*

*Or need some better specs.*

*The lass I see*

*Must surely be*

*From Generation X.*"

*Yes, still, they stare,*

*They're dazzled by her flair.*

*The sight of her sends young men's hearts askew.*

*So how come she remembers World War II?*

Around that time, while we were spending the week-
end at a place we had in New Jersey, Alice returned from
an annual trip she made to a plant nursery and said,
"Well, it's happened."

"What's happened?"

"I got a speeding ticket," she said. "It was the same
cop who gave me a warning in the same spot when I
went to get the plants last year."

"But I think maybe that's what a warning means," I said. "If you do it again in the same place, they're pretty much obligated to give you a ticket, even if you're an absolute knockout."

She seemed not to have heard that. "I guess I've lost my looks," she said.

"I hear they're taking in a lot of gay cops these days," I said. "We're all in favor of that, of course, but it's bound to change the whole equation."

She smiled. She didn't laugh, but she smiled.

# IV

*Having a family intellectual available, I can always
arrange to have words like "holistic" or "heuristics"
translated if it should prove absolutely necessary—
if they turn up on a road sign, for instance,
or on a menu or on a visa application.*

—Uncivil Liberties

Sometime in the late sixties, I happened to mention to an older writer at *The New Yorker* that I showed Alice my rough drafts. He told me, in an avuncular way, that this was unwise. He pointed out that the response to a rough draft hoped for by any writer, even one who knew full well the weaknesses of the manuscript he'd just handed over, was "Brilliant! Don't change a word!" Honest responses on a regular basis, he said, would be a strain on any marriage, and he had no doubt that honest responses were what I'd get from Alice. He was right about that: there were times when I could actually hear a sigh as she read a draft, a sign that the report was not going to be cheerful. Once, as I was leaving town for a reporting trip, I gave her the rough draft of a book I'd done on a college classmate of mine. When I returned, I found that she had written me a two- or three-page memo that made the case, in some detail, that the book would be much improved if I'd write it less as an observer and more as someone who had a lot in common with the subject. I pretty much started the book over again. When I was informed by the older writer that my marriage would profit from my being willing to forgo Alice's help, I told him that what he'd said made a lot of sense, but that it was too late for me to take his advice. I said, "If I thought that there was any chance I could get along without it, I would."

It wasn't as if I had married a biologist or a financial analyst. Alice had a particular talent for reading people's manuscripts and offering constructive criticism; she regularly did it for friends, including one who had written a sixteen-hundred-page novel. (She suggested some cuts.) She had a great eye, and, like Mary Francis, she was better educated than her husband. She had spent a year in the graduate program in English at Yale. She had copyedited books at Random House. She taught English and composition in college for years. She had designed the content for an educational-television series about the writing process. When she felt she had something to say, she became a writer herself, often on the subject of coping with serious illness. I regularly run into people who tell me how deeply affected they were by "Of Dragons and Garden Peas," a 1981 *New England Journal of Medicine* piece by Alice that's still used in some medical-school courses; or by a *New Yorker* piece that she wrote in 2001 about the decisions that had to be made a decade earlier after a collection of symptoms seemed to indicate a recurrence of the cancer she'd had in 1976; or by *Dear Bruno*, a book based on a letter she had sent to Victor and Annie Navasky's son, then twelve, after it was discovered that he had a malignant tumor in his chest. You could say, I suppose, that she was in the English-language business, and I was her sideline—the pro-bono case being handled by a high-powered corporate lawyer. That sort of help wasn't easy to turn down.

She actually did translate words like "heuristics" for me. Usually, though, what I was asking was more on the level of what some foreign-language movie we'd seen was about. "I don't get it," I'd say. "Was that a swimming movie?"

"It was not a swimming movie."

"Well, they seemed to be in the water most of the time."

Around the time Alice and I met, the coverage of American racism finally burst out of its regional boundaries; Northern universities were beginning to look into what they were doing to educate minority students who were, by conventional measurements, not qualified for admission. Alice got involved in a small program of that sort at Hofstra, and in 1967 she moved to City College to teach in a program called SEEK (Search for Education, Elevation and Knowledge), which employed remedial courses and tutoring and counseling and stipends as a way to integrate underprepared students. A friend of hers at Hofstra, Mina Shaughnessy, went to City with her, and for the next dozen years they were allies in the intense struggle over the role that a place like the City University of New York should play in what was sometimes known as remedial education.

From the start, some senior professors had been muttering about the decline of standards. As academic jobs began to dry up, some younger faculty members— people who had looked forward to a life of dropping graceful aperçus about "The Waste Land" to enthralled students on ivy-covered campuses—were dispirited or even enraged at finding themselves instead in gritty urban universities, correcting seemingly endless errors in grammar and syntax. Alice and Mina, who were there because they wanted to be, had a completely different response. It was encapsulated in the title of a speech with which Mina, by then a star in a field that hadn't been expected to produce any stars, electrified an annual meeting of the Modern Language Association, in 1975: "Diving In." Instead of throwing up her hands in despair at all the errors her students made, Mina had analyzed four thousand essays, found patterns of errors that could be addressed, and explained all this, in a tone of optimism and commitment and absolute confidence, in a book called *Errors and Expectations.* In later years, when Alice was producing programs for educational television, she'd occasionally take an unusual teaching job—at Phoenix House, the drug-treatment program, for a while, and for one semester at Sing Sing—and she always took it for granted that people who wanted to learn could be taught, no matter what their background.

Mina was fourteen years older than Alice—in a way a mentor and in another way a big sister. She had no children, and for our girls she became something like a fairy godmother; she once convinced Abigail that the necklace she was about to hand over had been given to her on the subway by a princess who was changing professions—getting out of the princess game—and therefore no longer had need of it. Mina was marvelous looking—the actress Maggie Smith was usually mentioned by those describing her—and she wore marvelous clothes. If Alice had ever been in danger of accepting the notion that doing good works carried a requirement for dowdiness, Mina's example would have been enough to convince her otherwise. A biography of Mina by Jane Maher includes an anecdote told often by the scholar and critic Irving Howe, who had become one of Mina's great admirers at CUNY: When she met him one day at the graduate center, having come directly from teaching a class, he commented on her outfit and asked if Mina's students, virtually all of whom were strapped for cash as well as for correct verb endings, were put off by her stunning clothes. "But, Irving," she replied. "My students know I dress up for them."

Apparently, she had also dressed up for doctors and nurses and medical technicians. Mina had been operated on for ovarian cancer at thirty-eight, the age Alice was when she was operated on for lung cancer, and I think it was from her that Alice learned the morale-boosting value of showing up for treatment looking your best. It also occurs to me that Alice responded to having cancer the way she and Mina had responded to what at first seemed the insurmountable academic problems of their students. Alice said in a speech once that the worst thing cancer can do is to rob you of your identity. Her identity included engagement and optimism and enthusiasm. One of the most negative words she could use in describing someone was "passive." I don't think I ever saw Alice just sit back and observe a group conversation; she was always a participant. After she'd had surgery and radiation at New York Hospital, she was discouraged from investigating what other treatment she could get at Memorial Sloan-Kettering; among some non-cancer doctors at that time, Memorial had a reputation for subjecting patients to debilitating protocols that might be more valuable for long-term research than for the patient's well-being. But Alice was accustomed to attacking a problem partly by seeking out the people who knew the most about it. Looking back years later, she thought it unlikely that the additional treatment she received at Memorial made any difference in her condition, but she liked it there. Among other things, she liked being in a place where the doctors had seen some people get well. She loved telling the story of encountering a teenaged boy in the elevator on her first day of treatment at Memorial. The boy was bald, presumably as the result of chemotherapy. "Are you a nurse or a patient?" he asked Alice.

"Patient," Alice said.

"What kind you got?"

"Lung," Alice said.

"Around here," the teenager said, "they treat that like the common cold."

Alice's response to having cancer was a reminder that an intellectual is not just someone who might be able to translate "heuristics" or someone who liked to spend her summers reading nineteenth-century novels or a pile of biographies of physicists. It's someone whose instinct is to analyze anything that happens and try to make some sense out of it. "Of Dragons and Garden

Peas" was not an account of the doctors Alice had seen and the procedures she'd undergone. It was an essay on how having cancer is "an embodiment of the existential paradox that we all experience: we feel that we are immortal, yet we know that we will die." She examined the talismans people with grave illnesses use to distance themselves from death—the magic of doctors, the power of the will to live, a concentration on the details of daily life (like growing peas in Nova Scotia, where we lived in the summer). They all had limits, she concluded, mentioning a friend who "wanted to live more than anyone I have ever known. The talisman of will didn't work for her." The reference was to Mina, whose cancer returned and metastasized about the time that Alice had finally managed to get back to her garden peas. After a year and a half—and eight operations—Mina was dead.

# V

*To state the provisions of the Alice Tax simply,*
*which is the only way Alice allows them to be stated,*
*it calls for this: after a certain level of income, the govern-*
*ment would simply take everything. When Alice says*
*confiscatory, she means confiscatory.*

—Too Soon to Tell

She didn't delude herself about the chances of the Alice Tax being passed, but she did believe that it would have been a good idea. She thought that, in a country where millions of children didn't have adequate food or access to a doctor, there should be a limit to how much people could keep for themselves—a generous limit, maybe, but still a limit. She believed in the principle of enoughness. The Alice Tax seemed to come up in conversation most often when we were with people whose incomes would probably have made them subject to its provisions. This did not surprise me. Alice had what I once described as an "instinctual attraction for avoided subjects"—a description I used in the context of a dinner we once had with a man described by the friends who brought him along as a "sugar baron." Somehow, by the end of that meal, the connection between sugar and rotten teeth had come up in conversation three times. If we'd had the misfortune to live in a milieu that called on me to work my way up in a corporation and on Alice to be the supportive and diplomatic and perfectly behaved corporate wife, I sometimes told her, I would never have emerged from middle management.

Once, I gave a speech at the annual dinner the Yale Westchester Alumni Association puts on to raise money for the scholarships it provides for students from Westchester. The other speaker was the governor of New York, George Pataki, who had grown up, in modest circumstances, in Peekskill, on the northwestern edge of the county. Although Pataki doesn't have a reputation for eloquence, he gave an elegant and moving speech about his older brother being admitted to Yale and his father, who worked in the post office, driving after work to New Haven to confront the director of admissions on how a postal worker's son was expected to go to Yale without a scholarship. (The director of admissions picked up the phone and called someone in the Yale Westchester Alumni Association.) "That was one of the best speeches I've ever heard," Alice told the governor, when he returned to our table and sat down. "Why in the world are you a Republican?"

She was direct. There were things she didn't like, and she was never shy about saying so. She didn't like clubs, or just about any institution that excluded anybody. She couldn't understand why anyone would accept an invitation to join a club, and the fact that there were people in New York who would actually go out of their way to get into a club just made her shake her head. Her attitude toward religion was somewhere between uninterested and hostile, except that she claimed to believe that you could hear what your children said about you at your funeral. She didn't like games—athletic games, board games, any games. In the spring of 2001, she had a bypass operation—the massive radiation she'd had twenty-five years before had eventually damaged her arteries and her heart—and afterward the surgeon asked me if she was someone for whom, say, tennis was important. When I mentioned that to Sarah—this was before I looked back and realized that this question was among the things he said that had begun to scare me—Sarah said, "I think you could honestly say that she's never played a game."

That was almost true. A friend she was fond of sometimes ordered guests to divide into teams for charades, and Alice didn't refuse to play even if she did grumble a bit. All of Alice's rules were subject to occasional exceptions, usually dependent on how she felt about the person in question. Despite her normal antipathy to clubs, for instance, she always spoke highly (sometimes almost covetously) of Tiro e Segno, an Italian-American social club on MacDougal Street; we sometimes had lunch there with one of her favorites, Wally Popolizio, a lawyer who had become, in effect, our surrogate uncle while we were looking for a house in Greenwich Village in the late sixties. She considered my membership in a Yale senior society terminally silly—she would have expected me to renounce it, or at least make fun of it—but when the subject came up I always had the feeling that she was struggling to be merely sarcastic rather than completely contemptuous. People we had come to know because a goddaughter of mine married into their family have some involvement in the cigarette business, and Alice, who could be frank enough on that subject to provoke a shouting match at a dinner party, never mentioned it in their presence. I realized that, because I thought of my goddaughter as family, they'd been granted a sort of family easement.

Easements on the subject of cigarettes were not given casually. Alice hated cigarettes. Cigarette companies did not anger her as much as those who did the companies' marketing for them by giving young people—particularly young women—the notion that smoking was a hip way to defy those square goody-goodies sometimes referred to as the smoking police. Given three overwhelming facts that she was always ready to quote—that lung cancer kills more women than breast cancer and ovarian cancer combined, that almost ninety percent of lung-cancer cases are caused by smoking and are therefore avoidable, and that the number of young women who take up cigarettes was rising each year—Alice thought that anybody who made smoking seem appealing was doing something that bordered on the criminal.

In 1999, a piece in the *Times* Style section portrayed a Manhattan "cigarette lounge" as an attractive and sophisticated and even sweet-smelling sanctuary where smokers, safe from their hectoring families, could enjoy a quiet drink or hold a private party—including, one waitress was quoted as saying, a recent baby shower at which everybody smoked. Alice was enraged. In an article in

*The Nation*, she wrote, "I have always been puzzled that anyone thinks women who smoke are cool, probably because my mother . . . was the least cool person I have ever known. I guess she thought she looked good when she started smoking as a teenager, but by the time I knew her she was pathetically addicted to cigarettes, always desperately trying to stop." In the piece, Alice mentioned that she admired Julia Roberts for working as a volunteer counselor at the Hole in the Wall Gang Camp, a camp in Connecticut for children with cancer and other serious illnesses—Alice was on the board, and we were volunteer counselors as well—but had to wonder "how many young women had started smoking because of how appealing Roberts made it look in *My Best Friend's Wedding*."

Alice had never smoked, but her mother was a chain-smoker and her father smoked cigars constantly. She didn't claim to know if the clouds of smoke she had grown up in were responsible for her lung cancer, but she was certain that her parents, who were exceedingly protective, would never have raised her in a house full of smoke if they had understood the danger it presented. She had testified to that effect in the late eighties, when the city held hearings on whether to ban smoking in restaurants—a ban that passed and was eventually extended to bars. By that time, she had allied herself with a loose band of anti-smoking crusaders led by the late William Cahan, a renowned thoracic surgeon at Memorial Sloan-Kettering, who was even more dangerous at a dinner party than Alice was, since he had access to X-rays of lungs devastated by cigarette smoking. In the version of her testimony that ran as an op-ed piece in the *Times*, under the heading FOR A SMOKING BAN IN NEW YORK CITY, she said, "I ask the city to ban smoking in public places because I want to do for my children what my parents would have certainly done for me, had they known what we know today." Actually, she hadn't left that completely up to the city. The girls were only four and seven when Alice was operated on, but when they got old enough to understand she sat them down and told them that, given her illness, we had to face up to the possibility that a genetic predisposition to lung cancer existed in our family. Everything else that could be a part of a teenager's life was discussable, she said, but cigarette smoking was out. She was at that moment at her bossiest, and both girls took her at her word.

# VI

*Alice's Law of Compensatory Cash Flow holds that
any money not spent on a luxury you can't afford
is the equivalent of windfall income.*

—Words, No Music

It's true that she tended to be the instigator of our family's money-spending schemes, but most luxuries didn't interest her. She didn't want expensive jewelry. She never wore perfume, expensive or otherwise. She couldn't imagine anything dumber than spending a lot of money on a flashy car or boat. Although she sometimes talked about how it might be fun to go to a chic spa and she always said she didn't see anything wrong with cosmetic plastic surgery, she never got around to either one. When she finally decided to buy a fur coat—she insisted on buying that and all of those other fancy clothes with money she had earned—she said that she wanted it only because of how cold she got during a New York winter, although the girls and I teased her by suggesting other ways of staying warm. She liked to travel, and she loved beautiful clothes. She liked living in nice surroundings. Her phrase for the opposite was "living like a graduate student."

Before we were married, she accepted the notion that she would have to make do with something like graduate-student possessions. "I had always assumed that writers were poor," she wrote in the article about her parents, "which at the time was fine with me." She was surprised that, through what she characterized in that article as "a complete lack of concern for possessions and a devotion to the clothes he had bought during his freshman year at college," her future husband had accumulated enough money for a down payment on a brownstone in Greenwich Village. At least Alice saw it as a down payment on a brownstone. To me it was just accumulated money. In the late sixties, nearly everybody in Manhattan lived in rental units. Co-ops were associated with a small number of wealthy people on the Upper East Side. The real-estate dreams of people who did the sort of things we did for a living were filled with roomy rent-controlled apartments. But I hated the idea of leaving the Village, which didn't have many roomy apartments, and Alice had a strong desire to own a house—not necessarily a house with an elaborate swimming pool and a basement bowling alley, but a house.

The brownstone we finally bought was not a turn-key operation. We had to deal with two rent-controlled tenants, which took months. For a while, we had what amounted to squatters. (When I saw Wally Popolizio to the door after he'd gotten rid of the squatters, he said, "Bud, you can sleep with Alice without asking me. But anything else, give me a call.") We had to do the sort of renovation that people in New York tend to describe as "the usual nightmare." During the renovation, I wrote furiously to keep up with the contractor's bills—above my typewriter I kept a quote I attributed to Voltaire, "Words Is Money"—and Alice acted as what we called the project manager. Once, after a particularly nasty scene with the contractor, she was sitting alone at the window of what was to be our living room, trying to revive her spirits by gazing down at the courtyard that had attracted us to the house in the first place. A quiet carpenter named Frank, who was working across the room on a banister, came over and said, "You know, sooner or later, we're all going to leave, and this is going to be your house." Then he went back to his banister. Alice often mentioned what Frank had told her. It was actually simple, she said: This was going to be our house. Our children, the first of whom we'd been hauling around to a series of borrowed apartments, would grow up here. It was all going to be worth it.

It has occurred to me—again, I've done no systematic study—that among married couples the person who actually makes out the mortgage check is likely to be more cautious about spending money than the person who doesn't. No matter where the money comes from, according to this untested theory, there is something sobering about sending away that much of it every month in the knowledge that, rain or shine, you'll have to come up with the same amount of money the next month and the month after that. I made out the mortgage check in our house, but there were a lot of other factors, some of which weren't obviously connected to luxuries or even finance, that affected the difference in the way Alice and I felt about spending money. I had been brought up in Kansas City by a thrifty grocer who was so wary of debt that, as far as I can tell, the house that my sister and I grew up in was not built until he could pay for it in cash. He would have been appalled at the idea of people who couldn't even afford a cleaning woman living in a huge house that had to be rented most summers to pay the taxes. In the article about her parents, Alice said that my cautiousness about money (she was kind enough not to say my petit-bourgeois cautiousness about money) made her feel safe—made her feel that she was not at risk of losing her house again, or having to rent it out to strangers. Still, she saw no reason to live like a graduate student if you didn't have to.

Studies are always showing that most marital disagreements are about money, but a lot of those disagreements about money are, of course, really about something else. In Tokyo once, Alice and I had a disagreement that seemed to be about how much we ought to be spending for a hotel room. I was on a U.S. Information Agency speaking tour of Japan, with a per-diem allowance—and not an amount that would have shocked the taxpayers. This was during a period when Japan was so expensive for people with dollars that one result of the trip was a column about how the main subject for discussion among Americans in Tokyo was how much a melon cost. I had inquired about the hotel recommended by the USIA people for Tokyo, where we were to spend the first few days of the tour, and it sounded fine. When we arrived, after a long flight, our room turned out to be spartan. Okay, very spartan. Well, all right: very spartan and small. Quite small. I started to unpack. This was a mistake. I felt a chill in the air. It lasted through breakfast the next morning. Finally, Alice said something like "You're just intending to live in that room for the next four days? That would be all right with you?" Her view was that my willingness to stay in such a room without comment was a rebuke to her. I was implying that she was some sort of privileged and spoiled New Yorker—more or less the person she looked like. As I remember, I had enough sense not to say that it's difficult to criticize someone without opening your mouth. Instead, I reminded her that I was an insensitive lout who wasn't terribly aware of his surroundings; in other words, I copped to a lesser included offense. Then we moved to a nicer hotel.

We once had a disagreement about how much to pay someone who was replacing the floors in our bedroom and in my office, the room next door. The contractor, whose name was something like Herbie, was a rather coarse but cheerful man, as I remember him, and I liked his approach to pricing a job: he looked over the area in question and then gave the customer a fixed price, not an estimate, of what the job would cost. When our job was in its final stages, Herbie told me that it had turned out to be more difficult than he'd predicted, so he thought we should pay him more than the agreed price. I didn't think so. Alice did. I told Alice that Herbie was in the business of judging what a job would cost him and then giving customers a price that was low enough to win the job but high enough to give him a profit. If he guessed wrong now and then—and I wasn't even taking it for granted that he was telling the truth about guessing wrong this time—he'd presumably make up for it by guessing right most of the time. If Herbie had found that putting in our floors required less time than he'd figured on, would he have suggested that we pay him less than the agreed price? In Alice's view, the point was that Herbie had, in fact, been required to spend more man hours on the job than he'd estimated—she did assume he was telling the truth—so if we didn't pay him more we were being unfair, taking advantage of him. What he would do if the situation were reversed wasn't relevant to our behavior. I said the world didn't work that way. Her world did. I can't recall what we finally paid Herbie, but, now that I try to reconstruct the issues, it occurs to me that if we had retained some Talmudic scholars to mediate, they would have decided that Alice was right.

In the discussion about Herbie's pay, she didn't resort to her final argument in such situations: "He doesn't have a very nice life." If I pointed out that some repairman's bill was obviously inflated, for instance, or if I said that I would never again enter a store whose proprietor had in some way broken any clause of my father's unspoken but deeply etched Shopkeeper's Code of Conduct, she would often say, "He doesn't have a very nice life." Sometimes she would add, "And we're so lucky." I don't think the Talmudists would go for that as a way of deciding disputes. ("A farmer went to Rabbi Eliezer to complain that a merchant had sold him two milk cows that, as it turned out, did not give milk, and, after listening to the farmer, Rabbi Eliezer said of the merchant, 'But he doesn't have a very nice life.'") On the other hand, she was right about one thing: we were so lucky.

# VII

*By now, my wife's policy on attending school plays*
*(a policy that also covers pageants, talent shows,*
*revues, recitals, and spring assemblies) is pretty well known:*
*she believes that if your child is in a school play and you*
*don't go to every performance, including the special*
*Thursday matinée for the fourth grade,*
*the county will come and take the child.*

—*Shouts & Murmurs,* The New Yorker

That description of the way Alice felt about school plays
was pretty close to the literal truth. Not only that: toward
the end of the article, I admitted that I endorsed her policy, on the ground that school plays were invented partly
to give parents an easy opportunity to demonstrate their

priorities. There was no doubt about her priorities. While our girls were growing up, she hated being separated from them; after a two-week trip to Asia, when they were about ten and thirteen, she decided that one week was her limit. Concerning children's constitutional right to sit down to dinner with their parents every night, Alice tended toward strict constructionism. When it came to trying to decide which theories of child-rearing were highly beneficial and which were absolutely ruinous to the future of your child—a subject of considerable discussion among some parents we knew—we agreed on a simple notion: your children are either the center of your life or they're not, and the rest is commentary.

After both girls were out of college, there was a period when Abigail was living in San Francisco while Sarah was in Los Angeles. When this came up in conversations with friends, Alice would say that if the girls remained where they were, we would simply have to live in California for part of the year. "If we want to be convenient to both of them," I'd say, "we could find a nice little place in between—Bakersfield, or maybe Fresno."

Alice would shoot me the look I associated with a catch-phrase from a radio sitcom I used to listen to as a boy: "'Tain't funny, McGee." By then, though, her desire to be near them was no longer based partly on her need to influence what kind of people they would become. In her *New Yorker* article about the recurrence scare in 1990, at a time when Sarah was a sophomore at Yale and Abigail was in Teach for America in Los Angeles, Alice wrote:

In the days after that bone scan, I couldn't find a hopeful way out. . . . I did manage to imagine uplifting conversations I might have with my daughters about how it was O.K. for me to die this time, as it absolutely had not been when they were four and seven, and I had foreseen their adoring but occasionally absent-minded father getting them the wrong kind of sneakers or losing track of their dental appointments after I was gone. Now I was sure that I had told them everything of importance I knew; they had understood it all and figured out a lot on their own, and were as close to perfect as they could possibly be. Then it occurred to me that neither of them was married yet, and I would hate to miss the weddings and the grandchildren. I speculated about which of my friends I would assign to help them pick out their wedding dresses. Then I cried and decided that I really wanted to stay around.

My problem in 1976 would have been much more serious than sneakers and dental appointments, I realized, when I finally allowed myself to dwell on what would have happened if Alice hadn't survived. The real problem would have been that I couldn't imagine trusting anyone else to be involved in raising our girls. I not only thought they needed to know everything of importance that Alice knew; I also thought, I suppose, that she was the only person who knew it. When I'm asked how both of our daughters came to be involved in the sort of work they do—Abigail is a legal-services attorney for children, Sarah is a clinical social worker—I, naturally, deny having anything to do with it. "I want to assure you that I tried to instill in them the value of selfishness and even rapaciousness," I say. "When Abigail came down to breakfast during her years in high school, I would tell her the temperature and the starting salary for an associate at Cravath, Swaine & Moore." But they had Alice there as a model. Because she survived, they were exposed every day to someone who (as a friend wrote after Alice died) managed to "navigate the tricky waters between living a life you could be proud of and still delighting in the many things there are to take pleasure in." Sneakers and dental appointments are the kind of things you can figure out, or find someone to figure out. Exemplars are hard to come by.

I don't mean that Alice and the girls were always in perfect harmony. Sarah, in describing the complicated relationship that she, in particular, had with her mother, said at Alice's memorial service that at the center of it was the fact that "we both wanted desperately love, approval, and admiration from each other." That meant that it was easy for them to wound each other even with an offhand comment. At times, Sarah said in that speech, Alice had told her that their conversations had made her feel like "a nerd around the too-cool cheerleader." At times, Sarah would feel that Alice expected her and Abigail to sail through perfect lives. Addressing that in one of her letters to the girls, Alice said that, perhaps because of a too-flippant family motto—"Pull Up Your Socks," which was sometimes expressed as "No Kvetching"—we hadn't made clear how difficult we knew it could be to get through the imperfect patches that occur in everyone's life. "As you get older," she wrote, "you will begin to understand that we love you not because you are perfect, but because you are decent and loving and honest and will always deal with what life brings you with courage."

Alice always said that parents had a huge influence on children when it came to what she called "the big things." Essentially, she meant values. In a letter to the girls, she once included among the messages we'd been trying to send them "to worry about being kind and generous to other people, to be honest with yourself and with others, to find meaning in the work you do, not to over-value financial success." Although we never discussed it in these terms, I think she believed in the transformative power of pure, undiluted love. Once, for the program at the Hole in the Wall Gang Camp gala, some volunteer counselors contributed short passages about their experiences at camp, and Alice wrote about one of the campers, a sunny little girl she called L. At camp, Alice had a tendency to gravitate toward the child who needed the most help, and L. was one of those. "Last summer, the camper I got closest to, L., was a magical child who was severely disabled," Alice wrote. "She had two genetic diseases, one which kept her from growing and one which kept her from digesting any food. She had to be fed through a tube at night and she had so much difficulty walking that I drove her around in a golf cart a lot. We both liked that. One day, when we were playing duck-duck-goose, I was sitting behind her and she asked me to hold her mail for her while she took her turn to be chased around the circle. It took her a while to make the circuit, and I had time to see that on top of the pile was a note from her mom. Then I did something truly awful, which I'm reluctant now to reveal. I decided to read the note. I simply had to know what this child's parents could have done to make her so spectacular, to make her the most optimistic, most enthusiastic, most hopeful human being I had ever encountered. I snuck a quick look at the note, and my eyes fell on this sentence: 'If God had given us all of the children in the world to choose from, L., we would only have chosen you.' Before L. got back to her place in the circle, I showed the note to Bud, who was sitting next to me. 'Quick. Read this,' I whispered. 'It's the secret of life.' "

# VIII

*The summer after her operation, I was finishing the*
*second of what turned out to be three books about eating.*
*The work I did on the final drafts of the book was*
*dominated by additional references to Alice.*
*The title I eventually settled on for the book was*
Alice, Let's Eat. *Spreading Alice from beginning to end*
*in her usual George Burns role was a way of*
*declaring, mainly to myself, that we were not accepting*
*the prognosis that would have made her*
*a tragic character.*

—Family Man

I was never able to remember more than smatterings of
what the surgeon said just after Alice's operation in June
of 1976. He told me the tumor had been malignant but

that he'd taken it out, along with a lobe of Alice's lung. I don't remember whether he mentioned then that there'd been some lymph-node involvement; I'm not sure I would have known what that meant anyway. After he had summed up the operation in a couple of sentences, I asked him about Alice's prognosis, and he said something about "ten-percent chance." I didn't quite understand what he was talking about. I thought I'd missed something. I asked, "Ten-percent chance of what?" And he said, "Ten-percent chance that she'll survive."

For some years, that conversation with the surgeon was unsafe territory for me if I intended to keep my composure. I couldn't talk about it, and I tried not to think about it. But it was the shock of it that I was trying to avoid, I think, not the content: for reasons I can't completely explain, I truly never believed that Alice would, like an overwhelming percentage of the people in her situation, die within a year or two of being diagnosed. Although she warned in the *New England Journal of Medicine* article that every talisman has its limitations, I suppose I fell for the talisman of will. I thought I could protect her. I somehow thought I could keep her alive because I wouldn't accept the possibility that she was going to die. I don't think Alice accepted that possibility, either. She later wrote, "I am known among my friends and family as an incorrigible, even ridiculous optimist," although she also wrote, "I was afraid that all the brave things I said might no longer hold if I got sick again." A couple of days after she'd learned the prognosis, I came into her room to find her on the phone, making notes. It had become obvious that the course of radiation would mean that we couldn't go to Nova Scotia, and she was trying to find a day camp where the girls could go while we made our trips to the radiologist.

A few weeks after Alice's operation, a neighbor of mine pulled me aside and said, portentously, "What she's got to do is to change her whole lifestyle."

"There's nothing wrong with her lifestyle," I said. I refrained from adding that there were some things about his own lifestyle that could use tidying up. He wouldn't have heard me anyway. He was off on a lecture about macrobiotic food or ingestion of great quantities of vitamin C or some other magic cure. What such people were saying was that we were suckers if we thought Alice was going to be cured of lung cancer by what they called, with some disdain, conventional medicine. Alice was more patient with such people than I was. At some point she'd tell them that her husband always said that his idea of alternative medicine was a doctor who hadn't gone to Johns Hopkins. But she didn't disagree about what they were really saying. "We got a lot of phone calls from people recommending apricot pits, or some such thing," she said at a medical conference many years later. "To us, and particularly to my husband, that was an indication that they thought I was going to die."

A couple of years after Alice's diagnosis, I realized that I wasn't thinking about it all the time. Gradually, we had found ourselves back in our regular lives. We attended our first family graduation ceremonies, at P.S. 3. Alice had become more involved in educational television. A company she and a partner founded eventually produced a PBS series that described various aspects of the visual and performing arts to children by building each program around an artist at work—David Hockney painting a picture for a program on perspective, for instance, and Max Roach working out drum riffs for a program on rhythm. I was again going on the road every three weeks for a series of articles I was doing for *The New Yorker*. After finishing the reporting for one of those pieces, I was walking through an airport to catch a plane back to New York when, apropos of nothing, the possibility that things could have gone the other way in 1976 burst into my mind. I could see myself trying to tell my girls that their mother was dead. I think I literally staggered. I sat down in the nearest chair. I wasn't in tears. I was in a condition my father would have called poleaxed. A couple of people stopped to ask if I was all right. I must have said yes. After a while, the pictures faded from my mind. I walked to the gate and caught my flight to New York. Alice was there. The girls were there. Everything was all right.

In the letter Alice sent in 1979 to Bruno Navasky—the book, *Dear Bruno*, was published many years later, in 1995—she said that at times she'd been angry at the unfairness of having become sick in such an unlikely way despite being what she described as a reasonably nice person who had always tried to behave herself. "My doctor said that getting sick like that—getting a lung tumor when you haven't smoked and when you are way too young to get one—is like having a flower pot drop on your head while you are walking down the street," she wrote. "It really isn't your fault, and there isn't much you can do about it except try to get the flower pot off your head and go on walking." That's more or less what Bruno did. *Dear Bruno* included a reply from him to the letter Alice had sent sixteen years before. It began, "Thanks for your letter. I really should have answered sooner, but I've been so busy. After you wrote to me, I made a list of everything I wanted to do when I left the hospital, and then suddenly I was doing it. There was high school to finish, then college. For a few years, I was living in Japan."

Alice loved Bruno's letter. For her, of course, the measure of how you held up in the face of a life-threatening illness was not how much you changed but how much you stayed the same, in control of your own identity. At least until the 1990 recurrence scare, we had gradually unclenched our fists and tried to think of Alice's illness as something in the past. Of course, we never completely lost sight of the dragons mentioned in her *New England Journal of Medicine* piece. In the blood-count line at Memorial, she wrote, cancer survivors sometimes feel like knights who have slain their dragons, but "we all know that the dragons are never quite dead and might at any time be aroused, ready for another fight." She thought the situation had been captured perfectly by Ed Koren's drawing on the cover of *Dear Bruno:* a knight, holding a syringe instead of a sword, is shown standing on top of the dragon he has vanquished, but a close look reveals that one eye of the dragon is half open.

When Alice's dragon came, it approached from a direction we hadn't even been guarding. In the spring of 2001, ten months after Sarah's wedding and a month or so before Abigail was to be married in New York, a routine X-ray prompted a doctor to recommend that Alice have an angiogram. The angiogram made it obvious that she had to have a bypass operation immediately— that day. As they wheeled her away, she was smiling. She said they were going to fix her heart. I had never before seen anybody enthusiastic about emergency open-heart surgery.

Part of that, I told friends at the time, was Alice's singular worldview. Part of it, I suspect, was the assumption that what we were in for would be similar to what we'd experienced four years before, when I'd had a bypass operation done by the same surgeon. Although the recovery had sometimes made me recall one of my father's favorite Midwestern sayings—"I haven't had so much fun since the hogs ate little sister"—it was, in fact, a pretty straightforward process. There was a steady, if slow, recuperation, and then one day I realized that I was fully recovered, grateful for the intervention.

But Alice's operation took much longer than expected. The surgeon said the radiation had made her arteries difficult to work with, and had caused some damage to her heart. I later learned that one of the young surgical residents was so concerned that he dozed in a chair next to her bed throughout that first night—the equivalent, I surmised with gratitude, of those traffic policemen who had given her warnings instead of a summons. After a week or ten days, she came home, but several days later she was readmitted to the hospital. By then, it was only about a week until Abigail's wedding. One morning, she said that we had to talk about that. She said that the wedding had to go on no matter what and that it couldn't be about her. She said it had to be the same wedding we had planned—the ceremony in the marble lobby of the Surrogate's Court building, the dim-sum-parlor reception in Chinatown which Abigail had always wanted, the same speeches and dancing. "No matter what," she repeated.

"We don't have to talk about this," I said. "We're going to have the wedding and you're going to march down the aisle with Abigail and me."

"You have to promise now," she said.

I managed to nod.

She got out of the hospital about six hours before the wedding. She did march down the aisle, and she was able to stay late enough at the reception to witness a twenty-minute or so rendition of the hora that left the Chinese waiters staring in amazement. The next day, she sent an e-mail to the group of people I'd been keeping informed of her condition. Most of the first paragraph was in caps: ABIGAIL GOT MARRIED YESTERDAY AND I WAS THERE. I WAS THERE FOR THE WHOLE THING, GOT TO SAY MY TOAST (QUITE MOVING) AND EAT CHOCOLATE CAKE AND WATCH BUD'S 87-YEAR-OLD UNCLE JERRY (WHO MARRIED SARAH AND ALEX IN MALIBU LAST JUNE) DANCE HIS ASS OFF WITH ALICE WATERS, WHO HAD BROUGHT ME ROSES FROM HER GARDEN IN BERKE-LEY. Toward the end of the e-mail, she said she was safe at home, in the Village, eating comfort food and about to watch *The Sopranos* and an A. R. Gurney play on television. She closed by saying, "Life doesn't get much better than this."

Four months later, speaking at Alice's memorial service, Sarah said she thought that Alice had toughed it out until she was sure her girls had married the sort of husbands she considered good for the long haul. "I know my mom's main goal in life was to protect my sister, my father, and me," Sarah said. "She wanted to protect us from worry, from sadness, from loneliness—things her parents had not been able to protect her from." She ended by saying, "Mom, I know you're listening somewhere, waiting patiently to hear me say these words: You were the coolest girl I ever knew."

A week and a half before, Alice had died of cardiac arrest. For a while, she had seemed to be recuperating—we were able to spend the summer in Nova Scotia this time—but in late August she began to feel weaker. She died while waiting in the heart-failure unit of Columbia-Presbyterian Hospital to see if she would be eligible for a heart transplant. The doctors said that her heart had been destroyed by radiation. In other words, you could say that she died of the treatment rather than the disease. Presumably, though, it was also the treatment that, against horrifying odds, gave her twenty-five years of life. I know what Alice, the incorrigible and ridiculous optimist, would have said about a deal that allowed her to see her girls grow up: "Twenty-five years! I'm so lucky!" I try to think of it in those terms, too. Some days I can and some days I can't.

## ABOUT THE AUTHOR

CALVIN TRILLIN has been a staff writer at *The New Yorker* since 1963. He lives in New York.

ABOUT THE TYPE

This book was set in Walbaum, a typeface designed in 1810 by German punch cutter J. E. Walbaum. Walbaum's type is more French than German in appearance. Like Bodoni, it is a classical typeface, yet its openness and slight irregularities give it a human, romantic quality.